THE LAST SEASON

THE LAST SEASON

Poems

DAVID LLOYD

TIGER BARK PRESS • ROCHESTER, NEW YORK • 2025

Cover artwork, "Displace: Snow Globe" by Kim Waale.
Cover photo by Sarah Cross.

Published by Tiger Bark Press,
202 Mildorf Ave., Rochester, NY 14609.

Designed and published by Philip Memmer.
Founding Publisher: Steven Huff.

ISBN-13: 978-1-7329012-8-5

For Kim and Nia

Contents

I

Earth-bound

Wilderness

Isaiah called out
where he imagined only God could hear,
beneath a blank sky, above a thirsty earth
indifferent to human tracks.

Calling for a path through the maze,
through a turmoil of trudging,
spirals paved with gold,
guarded with ballistic swords.

The sand beneath his sandals heard him.
And the flies in rock clefts.
And the seeds of desert flowers that bloom
once a lifetime—they heard him

within their knotted selves.
And all answered with miracles
of sight and sound that Isaiah,
eyes upwards, arms outstretched, tense

and unyielding, could not see
and could not hear.

Open House

What say we give up?
Fling open doors and windows,
leave wide the chimney flue?

Pull down screens,
rip the tongue from the groove,
crowbar shingles from the roof?

Burn fly-swatters. Bury insecticides,
pesticides, and assault weapons
in a steel coffin.

No vacuuming. No sweeping.
No sponging—not even skin.

Let dust roll its ghostly basketballs
across a threadbare floor.

Let stars invade our space,
downpours on mattresses,
sunlight on sconces.

Welcome the field mouse to the cheese board,
cockroach to the carvery,
bedbug to the duvet,
snakes to the wine cellar.

Birds swoop without concussion.
Raccoons scour the stovetop with quick tongues.
And everyone drinks from the toilet.

Give over to the ant's carpentry,
the wood wasp's spelunking,
the nesting swallow's mud-packing,
the orb spider's corner wizardry—

What say we leave unmolested
that drip hanging from the tip
of the blade of grass?

Worker

Nothing compares with the due diligence
of the carpenter ant.

She'll bite and hang on
though you're massed like a city.

She'll excavate the roof over your head,
tossing crumbs on your breakfast plate.

She'll hoist a wasp, ten times her size,
to the chopping block, and chop him up for laughs.

She reveres her mommy, would die for her, and does.
Rot is her natural home, webbed with galleries.

And honeydew?
Don't get me started on that sweet tooth.

She loves with her whole body
only her uncounted siblings—

which is why she's ignorant
of the extinctions of species.

She's not proud,
like me and you

with our elastic skin, hair gel, strategic evasions.
We love our mommies too, of course, but there's always

assisted living, with succeeding stages. Rot might be
our appointed home, and milk and honey

our promised land. But we bite
with slack jaws. We gnaw

with bleeding gums. We lift utensils
with subtle fingers, defecate

discreetly, no matter
which porcelain hole. We're not

like them, oh no.
Not hardly.

Consummation

I chainsaw a dead hawthorn—
sweat dripping, teeth biting,
wood chips pumping—and couldn't care less
about *Aprille with his shoures soote.*

I'm seeing an inferno.
How the dead are parched and silent—
husks needing a match.
I'm seeing heat. Light. Ashes.

I'm remembering February, convinced
it's my future—all that insistence
long since dissolved.
For the wheelbarrow's barrow, I raise up

a dismembered deadweight of trunk
that twists and feints and stabs
through glove and hand
with its sidewise thorn-dagger,

as departed as the tree
but present, having prepared its seasons only
for this.

No I in the Storm

Rip the leaves from the life's blood.
Fracture and fling branches.
Blast the clingy nests. You rule the air!

Congratulations. But I'm still here,
blowing and puffing myself.
Castigating and expanding. Ruling this chair.

Laugh, yes, I hear it, that gusto.
You banish the sun. The moon is gory.
So howl at yourself. Go on. All is you

or nothing. Do I care if you muster
from the sticky south a Caribbean fare,
your sombrero strut through sand and silt,

pelagics on the wing, rain on your back,
mugging clouds, sucker-punching peonies,
parading to my bunkered self, that's hurt you

not at all? Christ, have you no pity
for appendages? Then blast! blow!
I'm here, fingers drumming, toes wiggling,

my mind a private tornado, twirling strands
of air, lobbing memory grenades to Oz,
drilling to my bubbling motherlode,

terrorizing my land mass
with microbursts on the footstool,
flares in arteries. Dear God.

It's getting ugly.
The world isn't what it was.

The Unseen, The Unknown

You see me better with leaves half stripped,
midway between green and nothing.
My seeds are distant.

The creek and meadow—engorged
while my remains barely breathe.
Squirrels enjoy a bare scalp,

since any branch will do. But wrens need refuge
for their antic songs. Ruse of invisibility,
when wind bends limbs and agitates leaves

like thoughts that must be said.
But not for long. I'm feeling stiff
and can't accept this always-present:

each strip of peeled bark, each bole,
private ridge and notch in the sights of the sun.
My edges have waxed and waned,

adenoids and tonsils long since extruded.
So what's next, you ask, so edgy, you
with the eyes. I'll tell you. I'm not ashamed.

I'll push myself down, that's what.
To roots, to graspings
you don't recall, swirling tentacles, subterranean

touches, who knew? Though you caught rumors,
though you recite the muted forenames.
The dark, wet, needy, spongy, hungry, thirsty, reaching,

receding ends of me, tips and hairs, thinnest skin, intimate
with each squirming thumb of a thing,
burrowing claw, blind eye, hundred-legged

cousin, ring-wormed uncle, relegated
to always-shadow, the dead and the dying, yes,
the unseen, yes, the unknown.

Cows

Digestion takes forever.
So does staring at hills,
minute by minute shadings.

If cool—they lie down.
If warm—they stand.
Chewing is a lifetime project.
Magpies, their day-long companions.

Sex, a violent spasm, it's true,
but occasional, then the burden slides off.

Their massive, warm, hairy bodies.
Their slow, curious snouts.
Their teats filling with milk through the night.

Roused by the farmer's prod,
their calves close by,
they don't complain much, one field to the next,
tails flicking, crowding
to the never-long-enough trough.

When they turn their huge heads towards you,
they see you. They blink.
And then you're gone.

Beavermind

A low-tech lumberjack with all that treefelling, logrolling.
A sentinel, safeguarding stations of the pond.

Equipped for winter's depredations
with anchored bales in a soggy pantry.

Family? Certainly! Kits
groomed and oiled, cavorting in shallow safety,
slapping mini tails like daddy or mommy
when they glimpse the voyeur in the brush.

Social? Absolutely! Welcoming
even the skulking, ungrateful
muskrat to hearth and home.

But when is enough enough?
Enough wood gnawed, enough flow dammed?
Enough forest abridged to meadow?
When does nightfall's memory of steel teeth and bullets,
skin and fur draped over heads and shoulders,
dim to midnight that cheerful, bucktoothed face?

Never, I'm afraid, for the beavermind knows
this and here, not that and there. Which is why
when bats touch our faces and clouds inch like continents
over our heads, we need the beaver:
chewing trunks, stanching wounds in dams,
praying with dexterous paws.

Reckoning

Dew, wary of the sun.
Ant, of the woodpecker's tongue.
Wild flower, of any finger and thumb.

Everything knows everything
or dies. In blindness, the bats
assess my height, width, mass,

loping gate across the grass—
filed in the brain's cabinet
as they ravage twilight.

The doe surveys my gaze from the meadow,
ears and tail up, urinating, fawns stowed.

The coyote by the creek lifts his nares—
and I'm digested.

The turkey vulture reckons my age and health—
and circles on high, for now.

II

The Empire of Here: Sestinas

The List

Mostly raccoons, woodchucks, squirrels, where we live.
Moles, snakes, toads, possums, hedgehogs, deer also.
And surprises—those having no truck with roads:
bats, sparrows, pheasants out of time and place.
We mourn our dogs and cats, but shrug at the wild,
lacking collars. Watch out: big ones can stand

their ground: bear, stag, cow, moose, elk, bison—stand
and fall, fall and rise, dead then maybe alive . . .
And we drive on in our mobile spaces—wild
air banished; touch and wind screens, buttons; so
leatherish the seat, so cranked, "Rock This Place,"
rocking through fourteen speakers. The road

more traveled, the road-trip, *On the Road*,
road runner, Rhodes scholar, macadam to stand
your ground or back into if you've lost your place.
To coydogs: die! To songbirds: live!
Wyoming pronghorn, New York bobcat, also-
ran wolf, unlamented worm, formerly wild

parakeet, colobus monkey, newly wild
alligator flushed down a toilet—all crossing roads
that cross the Wild we bought and named—but also
claimed by them. For the flattened beaver, we stand
and salute. For the wounded penguin to live,
we donate. Arise, and go forth! We know a place

that cradles a crippled self, a place-
less place: water spigots, fish by the bucket, child-
proofed—keep on waddling: just please live!
We forgive the squashed skunk, and the turtle, road-
marooned, dogged, hard to know. Is he stand-
ing? Running? Helplessly armored but also

hoping, like those on this list I also
make of the night paraders out of place:
the drunk, the child, the stricken trying to stand;
the old, the blind, you, me—we all dance the wild
watusi with kangaroo, koala. Roads
know no fences, and no mercy—it's the live-

free-or-die wild card, vector and chance, so
dark, so radiant, this place that is the road
where we stand, where—for a while—we live.

Upon the Living and the Dead

It's been snowing for three days, with more
to come, each backyard stalk bent from a burden
of white. White shadows over branches. White
needles over the green needles of white pines
revealed each morning through my window.
You would think ours was a cosmos of snow

with none other to imagine. Just snow
and what's closer: ice, cold, wind. But there's more:
limping deer, coyotes crouching, frosted windows,
hawk statues on branches with their burden
of talons, hooked beaks: awaking from pine
to a still field to rip a mouse from a white

instant to its instant of death, also white—
clean as a flare of headlights, pure as snow
suspended, as unnamed as that white pine
born before I knew the words. And there's more:
all I cannot forget. The burden
of snow on a father's black hat, window

through which I see further closed windows.
My mother on her final narrow bed, white
sheets to her chin. The without end burden
of distance, our touching adrift in snow
that will not stop after more days, as if more
is what we need, human reaching, pining

for what will be denied. More. Those lean pines
that are figures of our love. The window,
a figure for what remains beyond, the more
that terrifies, as we yearn for the spent white
radiance of touch, smell, pulse, thought. Snow
that will not forsake us, everywhere burden

for shovels and plows, yet weightier burden
for our years and days. The tallest of the pines
trembles in wind, reaches for and gathers snow
onto its branches and needles. My window
frames that other world, not so far. It's white
and black, yes, forbidding. But I say there's more

than the transparent burden of window
or even that buried expanse of white,
green, brown, black. More than snow. Something more.

The Empire of Here

Now the cat's died—rabbits everywhere!
Lunching and dinnering on the gift
of mid-summer. And from nowhere a bird
descends to remap soil, discovering
the intricacies of grass. I could sit here,
emperor of all that's near, and not be

bored, or wage a war. Nothing can be
still but wood and stone while being here:
like the hummingbird that flits everywhere
without pause—though once it gave me a gift
of near stillness before rediscovering
its frenzy. Was it in fact a bird

or the flitting exhalation of a bird-
god? *Being and Nothingness?* or, Being
and Everythingness?—as in the hovering,
impossibly-aloft, loudly-everywhere,
nest-confecting bees with the golden gift
of honey. Yes, honey where I live, here,

primordial by-product of being—here
in this backyard, ignored by a songbird
endlessly praising itself: god's gift
to god, their chatty innerness must be
expressed each dawn, anywhere and everywhere
there's air. But now, here's me—discovering

my inner emperor who's discovering
he wears no clothes. That's right. In my skin I hear,
see, feel, taste my dominion. Everywhere
sex in the air or on blades of grass. Birds
squeezed into tight nests. Everything smells. The bee
dances to flowers and back, bearing a gift

for nest-fellows who surrender a gift
to the sweet-toothed. I'm discovering
ants climbing skin, how the landed bee
wiggles into a flower's fissure, here,
this place, where the picked-clean skull of a bird
dissolves into the earth. Where everywhere

is a gift for the emperor of here,
discovering skin, listening to birds
erupting—being themselves everywhere.

Apple Tree

The apple tree that I don't prune reaches higher
each year, pushing branches across
the path I mow through the meadow. Deer
devour the hanging fruit, believing
in an ancient promise: that a simple tree,
simply rooted, heavily full of itself,

will sustain them. Except when it
doesn't: one summer reaching higher,
wider, yes, but giving nothing: apple tree
bereft of itself. Frost had stormed across
the blossoming world in late spring—un-leaving,
gripping throats, canceling contracts. Deer

still walked the path that autumn, being deer—
scouring emptiness, until headlights hit
the eyes or a bullet the heart, leaving
beauty stilled, earth-bound. But now—higher,
the branches reach higher, fruit dropping across
to where deer open their mouths and the tree

bends its branches, as giving as a tree.
We forgive the past by surviving, as deer
forgive. And if for the next Christ a new cross
must be cut, carried, and raised, I hope it's
from an apple tree, raised higher
than any other—and the human who believes

when nailed to this cross must surely believe
in surviving past and future. The tree
holds that one close, as a father his son, high
off the deadly ground—no death for the deer
today, no grip on a graceful throat. It's
hope a believer tells me—that's what the cross

brings. But look: hope is strewn across
all battlefields, no ploughshares but swords leaving
rust and rot in the unploughed earth. It's
true that the world heaves with beauty: trees,
leaves, fields, paths, apples, the wounded deer,
the murdering frost—even that. So, higher,

raise the cross higher that all might see the tree
and the human believing, and below—deer,
hungry mouths open. Yes, raise it higher.

Because a Beech

The squirrel drey, wedged in the fork of the beech,
is a ragged mess. But it weathered winter:
the twigs, leaves, bark, moss glued with God knows
what magic—and with hope and despair,
and instinct, no doubt, when the reaching hand
touches what it must, just because.

And that's the point: the far and wide *because*,
god-wired into squirrel as into beech,
as into this eye and this blind hand
that feels past as much as present, winter
and the tossed seeds of spring. Don't despair,
those packed bodies tell us. Yet I've known

the still head on the pillow. I've known
fingers that will not unbend. Because . . .
because what? Because nothing. We're told despair
constricts while instinct opens. The leafless beech
gathers up tired birds; the now of winter
passes when seeds at last crack. A hand

touches another. Needs. Seeds. Far and wide. Hand
over hand. Mind doubting matter. Ear and nose
recollecting what the mind buried for winter's
deprivations: a thousand caches—because . . .
you never can tell. This week a beech
branch is a podium for a telling pair

of cardinals, whose instinct is to stay paired,
deprivation or no, brighter reds to hand,
or not: their own *because*, as the beech
that gives itself wholly—branch and fork—knows.
Because. What we don't know we know. Because
I know a pale dawn that shines on winter's

crusted snow. Because I know a winter
that buries a thousand fists under ice—despair
then hope, the frozen seeds bedded. Because
all things pay attention. Because the hand
that saws the branch rocks the cradle—knowing
no choice. So far, so wide. Because the beech

weathered its last winter, awaiting the hand
that awaits its warmth. Despair? Hope? Yes? No?
Because a cradle. Because a beech.

The Last Season

It's the season for small pleasures, when frost
bleaches grass, when wind screams its night name
and snow slowly reincarnates. It's a time
for lesser needs, diminished desires. We'll heal
our sores, splint cracked bones, warm our split hands
by flames stoked night and day. It's the season

for recollecting the early seasons:
when we slept naked, trimmed fingernails, frosted
our hair, lathered and shaved, our hard-at-it hands
like well-oiled cogs and gears, our nick-names
sloughing off our tongues. We ran, toes and heels
obeying all commands, no thought for how time

ticks a measured second-hand around time's
round face. But it does. The final season
announces. And guess what? It's OK. Really.
As when I step out the door to a frosted
morning that doesn't care, doesn't speak my name,
that covers greens and browns with pale hands,

vast fingers splayed, those rough, far-flung hands
that refuse to flex. I'm grateful for time
to burrow deep under the duvet, naming
what I excavate: crumbs, socks, loose change, season's
greetings, mislaid pets, the dustings of frost
in ancient caverns. This is the time to heal

the past, the future, the present, to heal
every instant of neglect, restoring hands
and feet—burnt white then black with deep frost-
bite—these fingers and toes, time and time
again stubbed, stabbed, fractured through all seasons,
my wanderings, my wayfarings, the names

I've forgotten, the names I refuse, the names
I speak as I peel back bandages. Heal
me. Forgive me. Forgive my seasons
of discontent. Forgive my frigid hands
grasping what they desire. Forgive the time
devoted to myself. Forgive the frost

its bite. Let me raise these now old hands
into the healing air, up out of time,
into this last season, this deepest frost.

III

Wing-beats

Miraculous Body

I was thinking

about Provincetown,
the lawn to mow, forms to fill,

a reception to attend, and the rip
a jet bound for Iraq can make in a sky distended

with God's angers, opened
like an apocalyptic piñata

to deluge the earth with frogs, gnats,
locusts, viruses—everything

humans deserve—when a hawk screeched
by Limestone Creek, and a cardinal asserted himself,

and the sky remained
unripped, and it struck me

that in a few hours fireflies would perforate the dark,
that bats hadn't abandoned us,

that grass masks grasshoppers,
that slugs would not neglect

their nocturnal appointments,
that the tousled, deep-red bee balm

by the window where I write
might lure a hummingbird so close

I could reach and touch
his miraculous body, if he would let me.

The Future Goldfinch on the Future Thistle

Goldfinch, *Carduelis tristis:* sad thistle seed eater

Because the flowers have gone to seed,
a goldfinch grasps a thistle stem to feast,

impervious to slings and arrows.
One's meat, another's poison.

But I've stowed the shovel, taken off my gloves,
shrugged a welcome to whatever rises

above the meadow grass.
Let the goldfinch guzzle seeds

into his golden belly, shaking others free.
Let wind lift those downy chutes heaven-ward.

Let gravity beckon with grasping fingers,
humming the good life down below.

Let air suspend them until
earth births them, suckles them,

releases them, that future thistles might surge
through grass, flaunt their slings

and outrageous arrows, that future goldfinches—
sad only in their gentle mortality—

might grip the stems of August thistles.

Another Truth

Lurching across the field—her best performance
of the Darwinian non-fittest: *kill-deer, kill-deer,*
waggly neck, limp wing—floppy

stick legs, the getaway that's no getaway
from those bit actors the turkey vultures,
or ravens on fence posts in faux nonchalance.

Follow me, she declaims, *follow me,*
you murdering ministers,
and I'll be brief. O happy dagger.

Claws, fangs, fingers, venom into ears,
kitchen knives, baseball bats,
concealed pistols with permits, pin-point drones,

raptors arcing from the vacuum,
the cubs whose only desire
is to rip up a carcass in the den.

All the world's a killing field, yet we know
or should know if we know the killdeer,
that other truth, that somewhere in this field,

she's stashed her eggs, far from where
the self staggers, chewing up scenery
until the moment she flies away.

Sovereign

The house wren is home
wherever he is

and won't shut up from the peak
of my roof, foremost lectern,

sheltering my home, as I call it,
and can prove to you with a paper,

though mouse scat
and that yellow jacket buzzing its death throes

on the sill attest otherwise.
But this guy, fit as a fist,

is sovereign over shadow and sky,
over papers and walls

and shingles that slope away
on either side.

Turkey Vulture

Life on thermals,
spirals like the dreams
of a dying man.

An eagle, you'd say,
from a distance.
Or red-tailed hawk
scanning for life.

But no,
turkey vultures are dangerous
only to the dead,
which they always seek,
which are always supplied.

They smell you.
They track you.
They turn their bald heads
and angle down.

Unleashed

On the pedestrian mall she snapped the pigeon's neck,
one crunch and twist
while the owner in running shorts chatted.

No throes. No blood. Just a space
between leashed and unleashed. The only gasp,
a mother shielding her child.
The dog? Proud then ashamed
when the owner yanked. A walk gone bad.
Will she fetch again? Will she wag her tail again
at a kind word? Will she again lick human skin clean?
Yes, she will.

Should one touch a dead pigeon?
Does one carry death wrapped in newspaper to the trash?
Can one continue after death?
Yes, one can. One does. One should.
The coo in the ear. The chat.
The puffed-out breast. The walk. So much to inhale,
desire in mouths, hands, paws, claws, beaks.
You can spay. You can neuter. And still we are undone.
The limp neck.
The head bobbing

like a wound-up toy, saying yes, yes, I am here,
on this concrete, this pedestrian mall, eating your crumbs,
shitting on your goddamn statues,
fearless and fearful, with no compass
for my desire, like your dog, like yourself.

Wonders of the Raptor

To inhabit a body built for the kill:
hooked bill, not lips,

honed talons, not nails,
a scream, not a hymn, eyes alert

for a tremor within ferns,
the sliding smudge in a stream—then,

missile in reverse, no remorse
for stab and rip,

flesh stripped from bone on the field
with black smoke pluming

from sudden craters, miséricorde
between armor plates, scavengers

muscling, the bloody boot print
in the grass.

Kingfisher Show

Everywhere I look, I can't
because this showboat steals the show,

paddling through evening air
with a priest's collar; crazed, uncombed hair;

killer beak, that blue feather suit.
Then, direct to a branch a dozen feet

from my front row seat
with masterful monologue: Death! Life! Meat!

No translation necessary! You're the star
of this spectacle, I say, but now we're

done, it's curtain call, take a bow,
I have dinner plans, HBO,

family time under a leaky roof
on my favorite couch.

But before I go, unscripted drama:
two deer leap a prone sycamore,

and my kingfisher—knowing
who's always king—

launches across the creek,
where my eyes must follow.

No Words

The parakeet says what you say. *Hello.*
Goodbye. Pretty boy. I love you. Good night.
Good morning. But what does he say

before you stumble to the kitchen for coffee?
And what after you've said good night and he's said
good night? Not a syllable.
Not a whistle. Not a sigh. Just the preening of feathers,

a squirt on the day's news. A shuffle along
the peg and back. A glance at the smudged,
oval mirror, though he doesn't recognize his captured self.
No words: there's nothing to repeat.

No dream of conversation.
Only the self, caged in darkness.
Small and wild, with clipped wings. Before you stumble in.
After you say goodnight.

Little Heart

A fingertip, the heart
of the ruby-throated hummingbird beats
twelve hundred times a minute in flight

and two hundred a minute at rest,
which it rarely is. No wonder
it devotes a lifetime to feeding the ravenous self.

When this creature mates
with a ruby-throated partner—
three seconds on a thin branch,

their hearts thump faster, louder even
than in flight, bursting out, almost,
from nearly weightless ribs.

Hawk Guarding a Deer

The hawk knows that hunger
always clocks in,
and a dead deer won't hang around forever.

So she stands sentinel,
taking her fill
with a swelled chest.

Nothing threatens.
Unless it's coyotes by the creek.
The fox beneath the barn. Vultures

above the clouds.
The hawk knows that nothing's safe,
not beds in high grass,

not sticks and leaves woven tight
on a branch, not tunnels into earth,
not the cooling carcass of a deer.

Safe

The grasshopper explodes
upward, sideways, upside down,
to ram through the dark

because who wouldn't,
cupped in a boy's hands then plopped
in a jar stinking of pickles and Clorox

along with ten brothers writhing
in a clump of wilted grass, the airy
walls too slick—

who wouldn't catapult, stiff
as a missile with every ounce of hind leg
kick and wing-thrust again and again

against the unbending unknown
while that boy with dirty fingernails
who screwed on a gray heaven

whispers through punctures, infusing
the air with Hershey breath and boiling syllables:
now you're safe at last

from birds and bees,
from girls who make you stutter,
and trees and lizards and spiders and eyes,

from men smoking in the woods,
from god problems bigger than algebra,
from parents everywhere but nowhere,

above or below or on the phone
or in the bathroom, you never know,
those somewhere parents.

To the End

Wild turkeys by Limestone Creek
hurl their bodies into air

as if they had a prayer
of flight: blurred wings,

scrawny necks arcing towards heaven
while the bulk drags down—

though somehow they skim the creek,
dropping onto the far bank—

like Orville Wright skittering to earth
after twelve astounding seconds

above Kill Devil Hills,
with all eyes up

and him looking down.

IV

A Table of Elements

1. Firmament

Origin of rain.

Backdrop for light.

Cloak wrapping exhaustion.

Theater for terror.

Cradle beyond reach.

Silence absorbing screams.

Dome through which to glimpse doubt or hope.

2. Water

Where there's water,
something happens.

On Mars. In your brain.
The cave's green.

Performances of paradise,
early spring, central New York—

orgies that forgot to say
they'd be knocking on my doors.

Accuweather promised "all clear"
when I fired up the grill,

caveman at home with flames and a grocery kill
in a world bereft

of mastodon and mammoth.
Fingers fussing with air-vent and grill-lid,

eager to stab with a stabbing tool.
Yet the commuting clouds didn't check in

with *Accuweather*.
Too busy mustering an hour's Armageddon, glut

of what we need,
pondered by Noah in his bone-dry heart.

Drum-rolls. Ricochets.
Steam escaping to a needy mother.

And I give up my paleo dreams.
Take me, take me: I open my arms to the big body

of the sky, which sees me
trifling on this earth—and knows me,

and answers in thunder, in lightning,
in ragged wind, and matter-of-fact rain.

3. Fire

The world is burning

Fire of the instant
Fire of the millennium
Fire fighting fire

In the core

Flaring off the sun

Detonating cloud to cloud
dendrite to cell

Flares from fingertips

In the widow's pyre

Across synapses with each memory
spark, each blink of an eye

Your hand on my forehead
Your hand on my chest

Skin yearning to become
wind or soil or another creature's fire

burning from birth
consuming each second

4. Space

I've stared up for six million years.

From when stars were microseconds
older than now.

Frigid promises. Reliable rotations.
Primal signposts.

Outlines of myself in earthly frieze.
Or so I believed

in my infancy.

5. Wind

In the calm before the tornado, trees are composed.
Wind sifts through the world,
shrugging airy shoulders. It's heard the news

on airwaves from north and west, where all that's rooted
is ravaged. But wind never cared for grip or gravity
or keys, or sealed windows,

or solids slogging on twos or fours.
The news is nothing,
for wind has seen it all:

the Minuteman silo's sludgy floor,
the fake turbulence of a Black Hawk,
the zero at the heart of the swirl.

Any obstacle can be side-stepped,
any mass flipped, any bird crippled.
Even these trees, close like a flock,

owning the evening, contemplating the years
like the great great grandparents they are,
cradling creatures within their compass—

even these trees add up to zero
when the ancient wind feels the spirit rise.

V

Stone Upon Stone: Translations

Iwan Llwyd

BORN IN 1957 IN LLANIDLOES, WALES, Welsh-language poet Iwan Llwyd is the author of a dozen books, from his 1983 poetry collection *Sonedau Bore Sadwrn* (*Saturday Morning Sonnets*), to *Sonedau Pnawn Sul* (*Sunday Afternoon Sonnets*), published the year before his death in 2010. In 1990 Llwyd won the coveted "crown" at the National Eisteddfod for his long poem "Gwreichion" ("Sparks"). His poetry collection *Dan Ddylanwad* (*Under the Influence*) received the Welsh Book of the Year prize in 1997. In its obituary, *The Independent* described Llwyd as "One of the most accomplished poets of his generation . . . ." He was a good friend of mine, and I undertook these translations in homage to his generous nature and his talent.

One Night Houses

It was widely believed [in Wales] that, if a man built a house *in one night* on a piece of waste land, he thereby acquired freehold right to it and to a small piece of land around it. It seems to have been essential that smoke should pass through the chimney by daybreak.

—R. U. Sayce, "The One-Night House, and its Distribution," *Folklore*, 53:3 (1942), 161-163. (Translator's note)

The worn-smooth stones—ice age litter—
scattered on the river banks:

waste and chips from the glacier's hammer
that forged each valley century by century.

And with that debris our ancestors raised a cottage
on a river bend, with solid foundations,

setting stone upon stone between dusk and dawn,
lighting a hearth fire before the landowner

could tear it all down.
Claiming earth, transforming the body's labor

into shelter: you'll see them on the banks
of the gray city's highways, in the concrete cellars

of empty skyscrapers, under bypass bridges,
in car parks, right now: lifting up together,

picking through garbage under the stars,
creating a home with scavenged cardboard boxes.

War and Peace

We all go through the stations of the night,
sometimes in an instant:
a flash of light,

faces glimpsed at midnight
having missed another train
before tunneling back to darkness:

at other times, hours slumped
on an empty platform,
a clutch of bags for company;

or yawning out tales of stale journeys
over a plastic pint of beer
while the next journey's skeleton

sings a round on the loudspeaker:
"calling at Birmingham New Street,
Stafford, Rugby and London Euston."

We all go through the stations of the night,
anonymous, unfamiliar:
retreating faces and embraces

hurrying past,
swearing under our breath
at the cold coffee or the body on the tracks,

screaming at whoever will listen
that we missed our connection,
that we're trapped in the stations of the night.

Refugees by choice, we have not known
the brotherhood of shadow stations
where trains arrive from Sarajevo, Colombo and Phnom Penh

to pour out tears from packed carriages:
where terror and pity converge
on the platform's pinball machine,

soldiers, journalists, wailing
families, garish cadavers,
a junction of weeping,

bursting, knotted up:
each alone, running,
yet wanting touch,

wanting to see another, to find
at the outer reaches of unloved night
one who is ready for talk, for comfort,

who'll reach a hand across the tracks:
we all go through the stations of the night,
fingering magazines on grimy shelves,

thumbing headlines, not knowing the sweet spark
of connection in the synapse
between finger and thumb.

Near Richmond Bridge

Richmond, London
April 2001

Once, at Walt Whitman's
New Jersey house
with its iffy parking lot,

I heard a poet-doctor
describe the exhale from infected lungs
as "a million stars shrieking":

so now it's hard to make an image
for the gray air of a Richmond street
on a bleak Friday afternoon

with planes baring their bellies
to the north
as they angle down.

I have no refuge,
no compass in this place
with rows on rows

of suburban streets,
the Audis and BMWs
chaining down the horizon:

even the lady selling newspapers
has nothing to say
about her headlines;

and the eyes of the chatting girls
in Ristorante Murano
don't dance the salsa

like the girls of Rio and Buenos Aires:
so there's nothing for it but to venture
into the heart of the smoke, and spark a cigar.

Aneirin

A poet of the Brythonic Gododdin tribe, Aneirin witnessed the c. 600 AD battle at Catraeth between Gododdin warriors and invading Angles of Bernicia and Deira, ending in disastrous defeat for the Gododdin. Aneirin then wrote one of the earliest surviving poems in Welsh—"The Gododdin"—describing battle scenes and the courage of warriors. (Translator's Note)

With camera and helmet
you dropped from the churning chopper,
close to where battle raged,

then scrambled, crouching,
for the nearest cover, bullets
and bombs shrieking around you:

then past the flaming bones of tanks,
torn-off limbs, bleeding-out soldiers—
raw meat, pickings for crows:

you slogged through mud,
sometimes rising to snap a photo
of man-killing in living color

or black and white,
in Catraeth and Kampuchea,
the Somme and the Six Counties,

with wizardry and craft,
and the young men flocked to you,
transfixed by what they believed

your eye divined:
fame that outlives battle,
hint of immortality.

While we endure

While we endure, the Welsh language will be a tough haggle,
a stubborn strata,
a promise on a pillow, a lie cleaving husband from wife,
a fevered night, boozy New Year's sing-a-long,
a breakwater for creeping tide,
beer having its say, cradle swaying,
shattered glasses, strand at ebb tide,
a stupid slugfest, a woman weeping,
a journey south on a May morning,
a street rousing to the day,
cruel money, raw iron,
a fog choking a side street,
a guitar strum in moonlight,
laughing children around dying embers,
fireworks, yanked hair,
crack of *cynghanedd*, flare of flames,
smiling smiles, sour grapes,
last prayers of aged men,
final hymn at the open grave,
blood on a palm, rust on a sword's edge,
a slick slope, a salty waterfall,
bursting spring in deep woods,
Zion on a hill, bedlam in the valley,
wheelchair at the cliff's end,
sunlight through showers, shrinking snow,
five o'clock on a Friday afternoon,
a locked cell with slave's shackles,
winter's freeze, wedding vows also,
a beating heart under ancient cairns,

love scratched beneath chapel pews,
while we endure, we'll depend, I'm afraid,
on taking suck from her stamina.

> *Cynghanedd:* the ancient "strict meter" forms of Welsh prosody
> (translator's note).

The Spider

With his web perfected
he lurked
in its sparkling heart

after a life spinning sunlight
for this circle of dew.
His labors ended

he listens to the rain
driven between strands
or dripping softly;

he listens to the river Dwyfor,
gray and uneasy,
complaining endlessly

on its journey to the sea
between rock outcroppings
and shaggy shrubs.

He had patiently plaited
the ancient, intricate patterns,
gauging the distance

between center and circumference,
art and artifice,
stealing diamonds from stars

to lure the unwary
to the stillness
of steel threads.

When a breeze arrives,
rippling through the netting,
he hunkers in the nexus of his world

like an old man under yellow leaves,
gathering all
to his composition.

VI

Enough

Enough

I return to the first.
Not Cain. Not Abel. Not Cronus devouring

his first born as Goya saw it. Not Osiris and Set,
the dismembered generations.

I mean the unnamed,
cracking nuts with teeth, spitting out shells.

Drinking water from cupped hands, on knees.
Knapping blades on haunches,

trimming clubs. Hunters of what runs,
gatherers of what's close. With parents,

with children. And somehow there's never enough.
Food. Water. Fire. Space. Sky. Stars. Flesh.

Never enough nearby or distant.
Enough nightmare. Enough fear. Enough rage.

Never enough muscle.
We hunt. We gather. We watch others do the same.

Across the valley. Across the river.
Cracking nuts with teeth, drinking from cupped hands.

On the savannah. On tundra.
Just like us. Knapping blades. Trimming clubs.

On our haunches. Telling stories.

Holes

Ever since the instant,
they're everywhere—

entrances, exits, excavations
sized to a foot or a finger.

In rock, water, trees,
grass, glass. Within are

teeth, food scraps, broken watches,
bones of the dead not absolved.

Holes that kill you
if not stitched.

Holes we're shoved out of, or burst into.
Holes for bullets.

Holes in one, in theories,
relationships, the heels of socks.

In Adam and Eve's apple.
And ever since that absence, we've prayed

to the fullness
settled into His hole in the sky:

Lord of Always, saturate our vacuum
with gists, flesh, hopes, flags,

rings, finances, putties, dreams,
banners, futures.

No Real Pleasure

Like all that breathe, the mourning
dove mourns, living a chancy life, foraging

the still-breathing earth for seeds,
bobbing its head

this way, that, there—constant
heads-up for the killing instant,

flying "bullet straight"
my book says, but can't escape

the bullet. Each year, twenty million
"harvested" like a continent of corn.

The oldest banded in Georgia, 1968,
shot dead in Florida, 1998.

Like BBs for squirrels. Like frogs in that upstate
pond I'd like to forget.

Roosevelt's elephant on its side,
Teddy's hand on the still-warm hide,

the other around his Winchester barrel,
mustache drooped, eyes level

at the camera while the elephant eye
angles nowhere. So many memories. So many

wrinkles in skin.
So much meat. So much blood sinking.

Like every conquest that's a window
to a damaged soul.

Flannery O'Connor's Misfit knew it
in his soul, and said it:

"Shut up Bobbie Lee . . .
It ain't no real pleasure in life."

Striking Gold

Yes there's swagger. Mouthfuls of silver dollars.
Towers occupied to glut. Yachts swamped.
Escalators and elevators grinding wheels, gears,
legs, fingers, teeth for the oligarchic sausage.

What's happened to words? Stained,
stripped, oxidized beyond.
Hung out in earth's spanking-new sauna.
Electrified in TV mouths chewing

on the bare wires of their fifteen minutes.
The declaiming of the "thing which is not"
until it is, or isn't, or might be, or is felt to be,
re-tweeted, amplified through the only

extant one-ton gold megaphone
in the national broken telephone game
until the end is the opposite of the start.
Or, that hangs in the air like an infected

blanket over scattered tribes. Or, that
blisters skin exposed to constant
airwaves, and who cares?
Or who cares who matters?

Or who cares whose lips whisper
to the golden ear? The make-great vibes.
The gold leaf that won't wilt.
Gold letters that spell nothing.

Gold statues in lobbies, gold drones,
a border wall of gold, gold fillings, gold gaps,
gold plate, gold pens and ink—
so much your poems are worth their weight,

so much your wallet rips through your back pocket,
earthward, defiling the water table.
So much your teeth glow,
an ache to the rotten root,

when your eyes reject what's in front
or behind, in the maybe or the finished,
and nothing reflects your face.
Shhhhh, don't point, don't gesticulate,

don't breathe about the golden warhead secret plan,
launched from a golden silo, detonating
inches above the tallest, hugest human
for the global bang for the nugget.

Say the word and it's clay in your hands,
and you are God, ripping out a rib, breathing out death.
It's breath, disappearing into air.
Gold. Gold. Gold.

*

But through a window this morning,
in the midst of green and brown and blue
and common air and threat of cold,
a goldfinch, grasping a tamarack branch—

black forehead, white and black wings, narrow eyes,
leaping its complete self
into the afternoon—for a moment
the thing which is, gold without price.

Earthly Remains

Among multitudinous trysts,
our dog loves carcass most,

indiscriminate as to species or status: mowed
flat, meadow-nested, splayed

on the wayside—
coyote-gutted deer, clawed sparrow, speed-

bumped rabbit, chipmunk
with tongue of blood. Cosmic

collateral or quotidian target:
no matter. To inhale, roll, luxuriate

in what awaits,
the I-can't-

help-myself dive
into the beloved,

guilty-gulping, leash-yank
and sharp rebuke

ignored. I understand,
I've been there. But the dead

pay no heed
to the breathing,

consumed only with
that trek back to earth

and air. They won't be
side-lined by

teeth, or tongues, or bile,
or sentimental

fabrications,
or inbred yearnings,

I understand, I do
but no:

for them it's down-to-earth, end-
of-day spewing of what remains

to the living room carpet:
transformed in shape, yes, but

not in spirit.

Earthward

Fingers that entwine with mine
as the mind drifts
down Limestone Creek.

Anchor for my ramshackle
cruise liner
with no harbor in sight.

Guide for Newton's apple
dodging branches and gusts
to a hungry palm.

A tug through rain and sun
like a mother who'll say anything
except goodbye.

But now I despise the pulling:
the thousand causes, the single effect,
that whatever goes up must . . .

the heart seizes,
the brain bleeds,
the bullet rips:

it's all the same
for the grip that tightens
and yanks and yanks

and earthward you go,
your entire self,
your bursting bag of memories,

so far, so fast
the arms and legs
don't even try.

The Maze

Caught in a maze—
one way in, one way out—

bends, forks, conjectures
about love and war,

and a stopwatch ticking.
Seasons change, the sky turns.

Did I pass this way yesterday?
Is the future a dead end?

Around the corner, Wordsworth's host
of golden daffodils.

But there to the left,
can you feel it?—
the psalmist's stormy wind.

Acknowledgments

Grateful acknowledgment is given to the following journals and anthologies which first published many of the poems in this book:

Blueline
Cold Mountain Review
Corresponding Voices
The Hopper
Nine Mile
Orbis Quarterly International Journal
Planet
Poetry Salzburg Review
Red Poets
Stone Canoe
Visions International
War, Literature & the Arts
We Not Me / Ni Nid Fi: radical poetry from Wales
Weaving Words Into Worlds
Wired to the Dynamo: Poetry & Prose in Honour of John Barnie
Zoomorphic

I am most grateful to Rhiannon Llwyd for permission to publish my translations of poems by Iwan Llwyd, which originally appeared in the following collections:

"Aneirin": *Dan Anesthetig* (Gwasg Taf, 1987)
"Near Richmond Bridge": "Ger Pont Richmond," *Hanner Cant* (Gwasg Taf, 2007)
"One Night Houses": "Tai Unnos," *Be 'Di Blwyddyn Rhwng Ffrindia?: Cerddi 1990-99* (Gwasg Taf, 2003)
"The Spider": "Y Corryn," *Hanner Cant* (Gwasg Taf, 2007)

"War and Peace": "Rhyfel a Heddwch," *Far Rockaway*
(privately printed, 1997)
"While We Endure": "Tra byddwn," *Far Rockaway*
(privately printed, 1997)

My thanks to Nathalie Anderson, John Barnie, John Bollard, Kathryn Kirkpatrick, Patrick Lawler, Margaret Lloyd, Phil Memmer, Linda Pennisi, and Kim Waale for their advice and encouragement.

About the Author

Poet, fiction writer, and translator DAVID LLOYD is the author of twelve books, including the poetry collections *The Everyday Apocalypse, The Gospel According to Frank, Warriors,* and *Shared Origins:* a collaboration between three poets (with Mike Jenkins and David Annwn). He published three books of fiction: *Boys: Stories and a Novella, Over the Line* (a novel), and *The Moving of the Water* (stories). His edited anthologies include *Imagined Greetings: Poetic Engagements* with R. S. Thomas, *Other Land: Contemporary Poems on Wales and Welsh-American Experience, Writing on the Edge: Interviews with Writers and Editors of Wales,* and *The Urgency of Identity: Contemporary English-Language Poetry from Wales.* His poems, translations, and stories have appeared in many journals, including *Crab Orchard Review, Denver Quarterly, Image, Massachusetts Review, Poetry Wales,* and *Virginia Quarterly Review.* In 2000, he received the Poetry Society of America's Robert H. Winner Award, judged by W. D. Snodgrass. In 2022 he received the inaugural Paula Svonkin Creative Arts Award. He held two Fulbright Scholar awards: at Bangor University, Wales (2001), and at Cardiff University, Wales (2022).

David also publishes literary criticism on modern and contemporary poetry, with essays appearing in many journals, including *Ariel: A Review of International English Literature, International Journal of Welsh Writing in English, Paideuma: Modern and Contemporary Poetry and Poets, Poetry Salzburg Review,* and *Twentieth Century Literature.* His PhD in literature and MA in creative writing are from Brown University, and he is Professor of English at Le Moyne College in Syracuse, NY. He is the son of parents who emigrated from Wales, and he grew up in the Welsh-American community in Utica, NY. https://www.davidlloydwriter.com/

Colophon

The text of *The Last Season* was set by Philip Memmer
using Minion Variable Concept.

*

Special thanks to the following individuals
who contributed towards the publication of *The Last Season*:

Carol Biesemeyer

Judy Carr

Michael Jennings

Georgia A. Popoff

David Weiss

More Poetry from Tiger Bark Press